THIS BOOK BELONGS TO

COMBAT PRAYERS TO CRUSH THE ENEMY

COMBAT PRAYERS TO **CRUSH THE ENEMY**

JOHN RAMIREZ

Chosen
a division of Baker Publishing Group
Minneapolis, Minnesota

© 2021 by John Ramirez

Published by Chosen Books
11400 Hampshire Avenue South
Bloomington, Minnesota 55438
www.chosenbooks.com

Chosen Books is a division of
Baker Publishing Group, Grand Rapids, Michigan

Printed in the United States of America

All rights reserved. No part of this publication may be reproduced, stored in a retrieval system, or transmitted in any form or by any means—for example, electronic, photocopy, recording—without the prior written permission of the publisher. The only exception is brief quotations in printed reviews.

ISBN 978-0-8007-6196-7 (cloth)
ISBN 978-1-4934-2833-5 (ebook)

Adapted from portions of *Armed and Dangerous: The Ultimate Battle Plan for Targeting and Defeating the Enemy* by John Ramirez

Scripture quotations identified ESV are from The Holy Bible, English Standard Version® (ESV®), copyright © 2001 by Crossway, a publishing ministry of Good News Publishers. Used by permission. All rights reserved. ESV Text Edition: 2016

Scripture quotations identified KJV are from the King James Version of the Bible.

Scripture quotations identified NASB are from the New American Standard Bible®, (NASB), copyright © 1960, 1962, 1963, 1968, 1971, 1972, 1973, 1975, 1977, 1995 by The Lockman Foundation. Used by permission. www.Lockman.org

Scripture quotations identified NIV are from THE HOLY BIBLE, NEW INTERNATIONAL VERSION®, NIV® Copyright © 1973, 1978, 1984, 2011 by Biblica, Inc.® Used by permission. All rights reserved worldwide.

Scripture quotations identified NKJV are from the New King James Version®. Copyright © 1982 by Thomas Nelson. Used by permission. All rights reserved.

Scripture quotations identified NLT are from Holy Bible, New Living Translation, copyright © 1996, 2004, 2015 by Tyndale House Foundation. Used by permission of Tyndale House Publishers, Inc., Carol Stream, Illinois 60188. All rights reserved.

Cover design by Dan Pitts

Author is represented by Leticia Gomez, Savvy Literary Services, and Raoul Davis, director of Ascendant Publishing.

21 22 23 24 25 26 27   7 6 5 4 3 2 1

Tribute

In every generation, the Lord raises up powerful servants not only to touch that generation but also to transform the world for the glory of God and for the souls of men. My life has been touched and transformed by these servants.

The late Pastor David Wilkerson, the watchman on the wall and true prophet. He was an amazing preacher and carried an incredible anointing. I praise God for his life and that it has touched mine.

The Reverend Billy Graham, an evangelist for Jesus Christ who evangelized the world. One summer night in Flushing Meadow Park in Queens, New York, I sat on a rock under a tree, eating a ham and cheese sandwich and listening to Rev. Graham preach one of the greatest messages I had ever heard. The message was

Tribute

followed by one of the most amazing altar calls I have ever witnessed. I was truly blessed, and my life has never been the same.

Nicky Cruz, another general for the Lord Jesus Christ, who went to those no one else would. His preaching has transformed my life. He is a true vessel of honor, an evangelist you will see once in a lifetime. His ministry has inspired and transformed my life and walk with the Lord to help me become the fearless evangelist God called me to be.

I thank God for these incredible men every day.

And I tip my spiritual hat to the Church in China and North Korea. Their courage and commitment have touched my life and inspired me to walk deeper with the Lord Jesus Christ.

Contents

Introduction 8

Part 1 Make Peace with God 13
Part 2 Dress for Battle 21
Part 3 Kick Fear to the Curb 31
Part 4 Stand in Your Authority 45
Part 5 Take a Warrior Stance 55
Part 6 Open Your Spiritual Eyes 67
Part 7 Face the Devil Head On 79
Part 8 Stand Strong in Battle 95
Part 9 Release the Thunder of God 119
Part 10 Cover Our Young People in Prayer 141
Part 11 Loose God's Blessings over Your Life 153
Part 12 Walk in Victory 163

A Final Word 171

Introduction

When I was on the other side in Satan's kingdom, I would have rejoiced at what believers are going through today. Satan has unleashed his witchcraft spirits in full force against the end-time Church. Yet countless numbers of believers accept the phony theology that if we do not mess with the devil, he will not mess with us. Really? Are we kidding ourselves?

The devil does not play at being the devil—he is the devil. He is looking to destroy as many people as he can and to take us straight to hell with him. And he knows that he has a short time to accomplish this mission. In the face of this, however, many believers today cannot even rebuke or bind up or cast out evil spirits of any kind. Without knowing who you are in Christ and

Introduction

understanding your God-given authority in Him, you have no authority. And you certainly have no fight.

Trying to engage the forces of evil without legitimate God-given authority is like joining the seven sons of Sceva, whose account is found in Acts: "Some of the itinerant Jewish exorcists took it upon themselves to call the name of the Lord Jesus over those who had evil spirits, saying, 'We exorcise you by the Jesus whom Paul preaches'" (Acts 19:13 NKJV).

These men went to church (synagogue), and their father was a high priest (which is like a pastor), but they had no personal relationship with Jesus the Messiah. That day, the demon they were trying to cast out made the ultimate statement: "'Jesus I know, and Paul I know; but who are you?' Then the man in whom the evil spirit was leaped on them, overpowered them, and prevailed against them, so that they fled out of that house naked and wounded" (verses 15–16 NKJV).

Even the demon understood the principle of Jesus Christ's authority in us. When the demon looked at the seven sons of Sceva, he saw nothing in them—and they got the most amazing beatdown. They even lost their socks. We know that the beating was so good that they had to go clothes shopping after that. Shame on them.

Introduction

This warning is not meant to frighten you, but to prepare you for the battle with all your heart. We need to stand in our authority in Jesus Christ and fight back today—not tomorrow—and be consistent and more determined than ever to defeat this fool called the devil. We need to confront him head on and stop letting the fear that he is all that and a bag of chips paralyze us.

Let us pray and battle with a holy anger, sending the fire of the Holy Spirit to cleanse and sanctify the pulpits and pews one more time before the Master gets back. Let us grab the devil by the horns—enough is enough.

Think of the 120 God-fearing people who stepped out of the Upper Room onto the streets of Jerusalem just two weeks after Jesus' ascension to heaven. Up till this time, the 120 had been hiding as marked men and women—with bull's-eyes on their backs—because they had decided to follow Jesus. But now, filled with zeal and fire from the Holy Spirit, they took to the streets and were confronted by an angry mob filled with hate. That mob included the religious leaders, the very ones who had crucified Jesus.

Yet they were not afraid to confront the devil face-to-face. They understood how to engage demonic op-

Introduction

position with the Word of God. When three thousand souls were added to the Church in a single day, suddenly this powerful movement called Christianity was untouchable.

Fast-forward a few decades, and already what started as a pure, on-fire Church had been infiltrated by the devil to water down the Gospel and pull people from the truth.

Today, we find ourselves in the same predicament. But a remnant is rising up, the end-time Church of Jesus Christ, and I thank God with all my heart for that. This remnant is ready to take on the last spiritual-warfare fight that the world will ever see. Many will be set free, people will be healed and delivered from demonic oppression, and every weapon in the devil's arsenal will be destroyed.

Too often we lose ground against the enemy because we simply do not know how to counterpunch the devil in the face. I believe that praying the combat prayers in this book will keep you ahead of any spiritual warfare that may come against you, your family, your loved ones and your church. Repeat these prayers out loud from the mountaintop, mix with faith and let every demonic force in the spirit realm hear you.

Introduction

If you have never asked Jesus to be Lord over your life, begin with this prayer:

Lord Jesus Christ, forgive me for all my sins. I repent in Jesus' name for every sin I have committed against You and everyone else. Please forgive me and receive my repentance. I welcome You to be the Lord and Savior over my life. Use me as You will. I pray this in Jesus' name.

Living boldly for Jesus does not mean that you are not going to go through hell and back. Maybe you will not live on the mountaintop for long, and maybe you will spend more time in the valley of your life. You might face trials, tests and attacks because you call yourself a follower of Christ. One thing I know is that the Lord we serve will never let you down, and you can take that to the bank.

PART 1

MAKE PEACE
WITH GOD

JOURNALING SPACE

I have made a decision to live armed, dangerous and out of the box for Jesus Christ. I refuse to embrace mediocre Christianity. I made this decision, and I do not care two cents what the devil has to say about it. When I first got saved, I took a piece of paper, and in my naïveté, I wrote a contract between God and me. It said, "I am doing life in Jesus Christ, and I want no parole." I am indebted to the finished work of the cross.

What about you? The Bible makes it clear that the only Person who can deliver you is Jesus Christ, not man. First things first—if you mean it in your heart to be set free, then you must also mean it in your heart to give your life to Jesus.

Pray the prayers in this part with me out loud, slowly and deliberately from the heart. Give them your undivided attention. If at any moment you feel uncertainty, go back and read the prayer again until it sticks in your spirit.

Make Peace with God

Lord Jesus Christ, I believe that You are the Son of God and the only way to God, and that You died on the cross for my sins and rose again from the dead.

"Therefore everyone who confesses Me before men, I will also confess him before My Father who is in heaven. But whoever denies Me before men, I will also deny him before My Father who is in heaven."

Matthew 10:32–33 NASB

Make Peace with God

Lord Jesus, I give up all my rebellion and place all my sins before You. I ask for Your forgiveness, especially for any sins that expose me to any curse. I ask You to release me from the consequences of my ancestors' sins.

For God has not given us a spirit of fear and timidity, but of power, love, and self-discipline.

2 Timothy 1:7 NLT

Make Peace with God

Lord Jesus, as a decision of my will, I forgive all who have hurt me, harmed me and betrayed me. Just as I want God to forgive me, I forgive them.

Make allowance for each other's faults, and forgive anyone who offends you. Remember, the Lord forgave you, so you must forgive others.

Colossians 3:13 NLT

I renounce all contracts known and unknown or any occult or satanic agreements. If I have had any contact with occult objects, I commit myself to destroy them. In Jesus' name I cancel all of Satan's plans against me.

"But thus you shall deal with them: you shall destroy their altars, and break down their sacred pillars, and cut down their wooden images, and burn their carved images with fire. For you are a holy people to the Lord your God."

Deuteronomy 7:5–6 NKJV

Make Peace with God

Jesus, I believe that on the cross You took on Yourself every curse that could ever come upon me. So I ask You now to set me free from every curse over my life, in Your name. By faith, I now receive my freedom, and I thank You for it.

"He shall call upon Me, and I will answer him; I will be with him in trouble; I will deliver him and honor him. With long life I will satisfy him, and show him My salvation."

Psalm 91:15–16 NKJV

PART 2

DRESS FOR BATTLE

JOURNALING SPACE

Are you dressed for the occasion to take on the devil and his cronies and to live on the side of victory? Are you dressed completely in God's armor?

Every time the Holy Spirit alerts me to a demonic attack, I meditate on Ephesians 6, going through the whole chapter to make sure my armor is on right. I believe that the armor of God represents the Holy Spirit because He is the protector and defender of who we are in Christ.

God has promised to uphold your place in the Kingdom, so you must protect what He has entrusted to you. As you call out each part of the armor, you will be putting the devil on notice that you have come to fight in Jesus' name.

Dress for Battle

Father, in the name of Jesus, I pray in faith, and I put on Your helmet of salvation.

The peace of God, which passeth all understanding, shall keep your hearts and minds through Christ Jesus.

Philippians 4:7 KJV

Dress for Battle

I put on the breastplate of righteousness—the righteousness of Christ Jesus. The Lord God alone is God, perfect in righteousness and majesty.

―᎔᎔᎔―

Blessed be the God and Father of our Lord Jesus Christ, who has blessed us with every spiritual blessing in the heavenly places in Christ.

Ephesians 1:3 NKJV

Dress for Battle

I put on the girdle of truth, because I know that Jesus is the way, the truth and the life. I put on the holiness of God.

"But he who practices the truth comes to the Light, so that his deeds may be manifested as having been wrought in God."

John 3:21 NASB

Dress for Battle

I put on the sandals of the Gospel of peace so I can stand on the solid rock of my salvation, who is Jesus Christ, my Lord.

Lord, you establish peace for us; all that we have accomplished you have done for us. . . . Your name alone do we honor.

Isaiah 26:12–13 NIV

Dress for Battle

Above all, I put on the shield of faith to quench every fiery arrow, spear and missile that the devil shoots my way.

Through faith [you] are shielded by God's power until the coming of the salvation that is ready to be revealed in the last time.

1 Peter 1:5 NIV

Dress for Battle

Lord, I pick up the precious sword of the Spirit to slice and dice with the power of the Holy Spirit any assault of the evil one against me. I stand all the days of my life on offense and on defense, in Jesus' name.

God's purpose in all this was to use the church to display his wisdom in its rich variety to all the unseen rulers and authorities in the heavenly places. This was his eternal plan, which he carried out through Christ Jesus our Lord.

Ephesians 3:10–11 NLT

Dress for Battle

Father, I ask You to surround my loved ones and me with a supernatural wall of fire. In the unmatchable name of Jesus, I stand dressed in the armor of God and claim Your promise to be my protector always.

For though we walk in the flesh, we do not war according to the flesh. For the weapons of our warfare are not carnal but mighty in God for pulling down strongholds.

2 Corinthians 10:3–4 NKJV

PART 3

KICK FEAR
TO THE CURB

JOURNALING SPACE

Before you go into battle, you must get rid of all fear, doubt and unbelief. These will hinder you. Do not be held back by self-consciousness or embarrassment of any kind, because at that point the devil can attack and make you believe that deliverance is not going to happen.

You need to understand two things: Our God is great, and the devil is limited. God has already given you the victory. You just need to step into it and take it from the devil's hands—the same way that God gave the children of Israel the Promised Land, but they had to go in there and take it.

I stand against the spirit of fear that is trying to operate in my life. I refuse to accept and operate in fear. I uproot it, in the name of Jesus.

Be strong in the Lord, and in the power of his might.

Ephesians 6:10 KJV

Right now, I bind any demonic powers that are trying to take over my mind, my thinking and my heart. I dismantle them in the name of Jesus Christ.

You, O Lord, are a shield about me, my glory, and the lifter of my head.

Psalm 3:3 ESV

With the blood of Jesus Christ and the finished work of the cross, I uproot all tormenting and scorning spirits that have implanted themselves in my mind and thoughts. I call back from the north, the south, the east and the west every fragmented piece of my mind—I call them back in the name of Jesus. I speak to my mind to be whole, healed and delivered out of the enemy's hands, in Jesus' name.

"Who has known the mind of the Lord so as to instruct him?" But we have the mind of Christ.

1 Corinthians 2:16 NIV

I reject every evil report—infirmity, broken relationship, loss of job, loss of loved one—that is trying to bring fear into my life. I destroy it in Jesus' name.

Yet in all these things we are more than conquerors through Him who loved us.

Romans 8:37 NKJV

Kick Fear to the Curb

I declare and decree that no weapon formed against me will prosper, in Jesus' name. I loose my family and myself from a spirit of fear that is trying to paralyze me.

"Therefore if the Son makes you free, you shall be free indeed."

John 8:36 NKJV

Kick Fear to the Curb

I bind the spirit of fear of man, fear of people and fear of those in authority over me. I uproot that spirit of fear, in the name of Jesus. Lord, I declare over my life that You are my shield and protector, in Jesus' name.

Then [one who resembled a human being] said to me, "Do not be afraid, Daniel, for from the first day that you set your heart on understanding this and on humbling yourself before you God, your words were heard, and I have come in response to your words."

Daniel 10:12 NASB

Lord Jesus, no matter what comes my way, I make a decision to trust You in every area of my life.

Weeping may endure for a night, but joy cometh in the morning.

Psalm 30:5 KJV

Kick Fear to the Curb

If God is for me, who can be against me?

Yes, the LORD is for me; he will help me. I will look in triumph at those who hate me. . . . They swarmed around me like bees; they blazed against me like a crackling fire. But I destroyed them all with the authority of the LORD.

Psalm 118:7, 12 NLT

I cover my family, my ministry and myself in the blood of Jesus Christ.

For I know the thoughts that I think toward you, says the LORD, thoughts of peace and not of evil, to give you a future and a hope.

Jeremiah 29:11 NKJV

I cover my mind and my sleep in the blood of my Savior, Jesus Christ.

I lay down and slept, yet I woke up in safety, for the LORD was watching over me.

Psalm 3:5 NLT

Kick Fear to the Curb

Father, in the name of Jesus, I ask You to send a host of ministering angels to attend to my hurts and my needs, and to strengthen me in every season of my life.

"Because he has loved Me, therefore I will deliver him; I will set him securely on high, because he has known My name. He will call upon Me, and I will answer him; I will be with him in trouble; I will rescue him and honor him. With a long life I will satisfy him and let him see My salvation."

Psalm 91:14–16 NASB

PART 4

STAND IN YOUR AUTHORITY

JOURNALING SPACE

Do not let the devil play you and draw you into his game. Stop fighting the devil and his cronies from where he is in his low position, because he is not higher than our Lord Jesus Christ. We attack him from our position of authority seated with Jesus in the highest heavens at the right hand of God the Father.

As the Church of Jesus Christ, which He left on the earth to represent His name, we are empowered to take down demonic strongholds, defeat the devil's game plan, go into the devil's territory without fear and wreak havoc. We do all this by our God-given authority that Jesus won for us at the cross.

There is victory yesterday, today, tomorrow and forevermore.

I am an overcomer in Christ Jesus. I declare and decree that I cannot fail.

God raised us up with Christ and seated us with him in the heavenly realms in Christ Jesus.

Ephesians 2:6 NIV

Stand in Your Authority

I declare and decree that no weapon formed against me shall prosper. Only the Lord's plans for my life will prosper, in Jesus' name.

"Call upon Me in the day of trouble; I will deliver you, and you shall glorify Me."

Psalm 50:15 NKJV

Stand in Your Authority

I declare and decree that I am triumphant in every season of my life, in Jesus' name.

The LORD will make you the head, not the tail. If you pay attention to the commands of the LORD your God that I give you this day and carefully follow them, you will always be at the top, never at the bottom.

Deuteronomy 28:13 NIV

Stand in Your Authority

I declare and decree that I turn back every negative arrow that is against me and send it to the enemy's camp, in Jesus' name.

Surely He shall deliver you from the snare of the fowler and from the perilous pestilence. He shall cover you with His feathers, and under His wings you shall take refuge.

Psalm 91:3–4 NKJV

Stand in Your Authority

I declare and decree that every fiery dart of the enemy against me today is quenched, in the name of Jesus.

You shall not be afraid of the terror by night, nor of the arrow that flies by day, nor of the pestilence that walks in darkness, nor of the destruction that lays waste at noonday.

Psalm 91:5–6 NKJV

Today I declare and decree that I am victorious and an overcomer because greater is He that lives in me than he that lives in the world. Thank You, Jesus.

Therefore God also has highly exalted [Jesus] and given Him the name which is above every name, that at the name of Jesus every knee should bow, of those in heaven, and of those on earth, and of those under the earth,

Philippians 2:9–10 NKJV

Stand in Your Authority

Lord Jesus, I want to thank You for my victory and Your promises, because through these prayers I take the offensive position by the power of the Holy Spirit who lives in me and by the anointing that You placed upon my life. Today, I declare and decree that I am a champion in Jesus Christ.

Hath he spoken, and shall he not make it good?

Numbers 23:19 KJV

PART 5

TAKE A WARRIOR STANCE

JOURNALING SPACE

The Spirit of God gives life and liberty; Satan seeks only to kill, steal and destroy—and, in the process, to control you.

This is a tragedy. It does not have to end that way for anyone.

Please hear me. I am an ex–devil worshiper, a former general in the devil's kingdom, sounding the trumpet so that you can get out and be set free—both you and your family. It is time to get radical. Let us no longer be stagnant, seeker friendly and politically correct. None of these will chase the devil away. Let us rise up as the Church and cause God's enemies to be scattered.

As you pray these prayers of equipping, you will be joining with the end-time Church that Jesus Christ is coming back for. You will be positioning yourself as a spiritual sniper in order to bring down targets in the enemy's camp as you never have before.

Take a Warrior Stance

Father, I pick up the weapons of my warfare. By the blood of Jesus Christ, I stand in the devil's face in this battle.

Therefore, this is what the Sovereign LORD says: "Look! I am placing a foundation stone in Jerusalem, a firm and tested stone. It is a precious cornerstone that is safe to build on. Whoever believes need never be shaken."

Isaiah 28:16 NLT

Take a Warrior Stance

I cover my spirit, my body, my mind, my will and my emotions in the blood of Jesus. I cover my family in the blood of Jesus Christ. I cover my job and my career in the blood of Jesus Christ. I cover my vehicle in the blood of Jesus and claim protection from any accidents. I decree victory over my finances, in Jesus' name. I pray the Lord will release angels from Michael's quarters to stand guard in my home in the name of Jesus Christ.

And [Jesus] said to them, . . . "Behold, I have given you authority . . . over all the power of the enemy, and nothing will injure you."

Luke 10:18–19 NASB

Take a Warrior Stance

I call upon the Holy Spirit right now to make me invisible in the spirit realm, as well as my family, my ministry and my loved ones, so that the devil and his demons cannot find me.

[The Lord] will conceal me . . . when troubles come; he will hide me in his sanctuary. He will place me out of reach on a high rock. Then I will hold my head high above my enemies who surround me.

Psalm 27:5–6 NLT

Take a Warrior Stance

I seal my family, my ministry and my church in the blood of Jesus Christ and declare a wall of fire around them. I ask You, Lord, to keep the same hedge of protection around my family, my mind, my heart, my emotions, my ministry and my relationship with You that you put around Job.

Satan answered the LORD and said, . . . "Have you not put a hedge around him and his house and all that he has, on every side? You have blessed the work of his hands, and his possessions have increased in the land."

Job 1:9–10 ESV

Take a Warrior Stance

I profess and declare in the name of Jesus that I have the mind of Christ. I will have good memory and a sharp mind, because the battlefield is in the mind.

Thou wilt keep him in perfect peace, whose mind is stayed on thee.

Isaiah 26:3 KJV

Take a Warrior Stance

I pray that every time I lay down my head, I will have good sleep, in Jesus' name.

Where morning dawns, where evening fades, you call forth songs of joy.

Psalm 65:8 NIV

Take a Warrior Stance

I ask the Lord to equip me with wisdom and knowledge, in Jesus' name. I ask Jesus Christ to fill me with the fruit of the Spirit: love, joy, peace, patience, kindness, goodness, faithfulness, gentleness and self-control.

[Jesus said,] "Behold, I am sending you out as sheep in the midst of wolves, so be wise as serpents and innocent as doves."

Matthew 10:16 ESV

Take a Warrior Stance

I pray God's favor and grace over my life, in Jesus' name. I pray God's mercy over my life, in the name of Jesus. I pray spiritual hearing and spiritual sight over my life; I pray that the revelation of God's love be engrafted in my heart, in Jesus' name.

And He will arise and shepherd His flock in the strength of the LORD, in the majesty of the name of the LORD His God. And they will remain, because at that time He will be great to the ends of the earth. This One will be our peace.

Micah 5:4–5 NASB

Take a Warrior Stance

I declare peace and joy over my life, in Jesus' name. I will seek an intimate relationship with Jesus all the days of my life.

"Because he has set his love upon Me, therefore I will deliver him; I will set him on high, because he has known My name."

Psalm 91:14 NKJV

PART 6

OPEN YOUR SPIRITUAL EYES

JOURNALING SPACE

There is no way that we can be effective in the spirit realm without having discernment of the supernatural. If you can understand the supernatural, you can walk in the supernatural; your spiritual eyes have to be open at all times. This truth is more important in our Christian walk than the oxygen we breathe.

So I want to share the following prayer points with you. These prayers will help open your spiritual eyes to see in the spirit realm what God wants you to see. I know they are going to bless you—and your life will never be the same.

Open Your Spiritual Eyes

Lord, in Jesus' name, I ask You to remove every spiritual distraction and the scales that have blinded me from seeing in the Spirit.

Thou hast delivered my soul from death: wilt not thou deliver my feet from falling, that I may walk before God in the light of the living?

Psalm 56:13 KJV

Open Your Spiritual Eyes

Holy Spirit, in the name of Jesus, open my spiritual eyes to see what my natural eyes cannot. Let me see into the spirit realm with understanding.

> "To God belong wisdom and power; counsel and understanding are his. . . . He reveals the deep things of darkness and brings utter darkness into the light."
>
> Job 12:13, 22 NIV

Open Your Spiritual Eyes

I ask the Holy Spirit, in the name of Jesus, to give me insight into the evil plans of the witches, the sorcerers and the warlocks that are against my family, my ministry and my life.

The Lord is known by the judgment He executes; the wicked is snared in the work of his own hands.

Psalm 9:16 NKJV

Open Your Spiritual Eyes

Lord, bless my eyes to see every entrapment of the evil one that is trying to come against me, in Jesus' name. Holy Spirit, help me discern the things that I do not understand and cannot see.

May [the wicked] disappear like water into thirsty ground. Make their weapons useless in their hands. . . . The godly will rejoice when they see injustice avenged.

Psalm 58:7, 10 NLT

Open Your Spiritual Eyes

Holy Spirit, equip me with spiritual wisdom, in Jesus' name. Holy Spirit, I pray for spiritual knowledge, in Jesus' name.

I pray for you constantly, asking God, the glorious Father of our Lord Jesus Christ, to give you spiritual wisdom and insight so that you might grow in your knowledge of God.

Ephesians 1:16–17 NLT

Open Your Spiritual Eyes

Holy Spirit, in the name of Jesus, reveal to me the mysteries of the Kingdom.

The word of God, that is, the mystery which has been hidden from the past ages and generations . . . has now been manifested to His saints.

Colossians 1:25–26 NASB

Lord, show me how to be a blessing to the Body of Christ as You open my spiritual eyes to the understanding of Your Word, in Jesus' name.

And the Lord make you to increase and abound in love one toward another . . . to the end he may stablish your hearts unblameable in holiness before God, even our Father.

1 Thessalonians 3:12–13 KJV

Open Your Spiritual Eyes

I pray in the name of Jesus, Lord, please use my gifts to be a blessing to others in my walk with You. I speak into my ministry spiritual vision and revelation, in Jesus' name.

I will sing of the mercies of the LORD forever; with my mouth will I make known Your faithfulness to all generations. For I have said, "Mercy shall be built up forever; your faithfulness You shall establish in the very heavens."

Psalm 89:1–2 NKJV

Open Your Spiritual Eyes

Lord Jesus, open my spiritual eyes to see all the great things that You have for me. Never let the light in my eyes go out, in Jesus' name.

I pray that your hearts will be flooded with light so that you can understand the confident hope he has given to those he called—his holy people who are his rich and glorious inheritance.

Ephesians 1:18 NLT

PART 7

FACE THE DEVIL HEAD ON

JOURNALING SPACE

It is time the Church take the offensive position, with our quivers full of arrows dipped in the blood of Jesus, shooting into the enemy's camp to destroy every evil target and taking our position of authority seated with Christ Jesus in the highest heaven (see Ephesians 2:6).

In this way, we send confusion into the enemy's camp and change the languages of the evil ones so they cannot communicate with one another. Doing this leads to the shutting down of the first and second heavens where the principalities distribute their orders to the territorial demons in the earth realm. We burn their banners and scrolls with the fire of the Holy Spirit. The banners represent their position, and the scrolls dictate what assignment they have against us.

In this part, I will teach you how to take back everything the enemy has stolen from you. We must tell the devil to his face that we are cutting ties and legal rights, and burning with the fire of the Holy Spirit every agreement we have unwittingly made with him.

We are going to show the devil that he picked the wrong Christians to mess with because we are not afraid.

Face the Devil Head On

Satan, listen to me right now. I alone cannot stop what you throw at me, but one thing I know: I can do something about it through my Lord Jesus Christ. I know my God is able. The Bible says, "Now unto him that is able to do exceeding abundantly above all that we ask or think, according to the power that worketh in us, unto him be glory" (Ephesians 3:20–21 KJV). I will stand on that Word for me and my house.

"[God] will guard the feet of his faithful ones, but the wicked shall be cut off in darkness."

1 Samuel 2:9 ESV

Face the Devil Head On

I break every demonic altar that has been set up in the spirit realm against my family, my loved ones, my ministry and me; I destroy them in the name of Jesus Christ. I paralyze every demon who has been assigned to me in the season I am in now.

I also pray that you will understand the incredible greatness of God's power for us who believe him. This is the same mighty power that raised Christ from the dead.

Ephesians 1:19–20 NLT

Face the Devil Head On

I uproot every incantation and spiritual roadblock that the enemy has set against me. I pulverize every attack against me, and I curse it at the root, never to return, in the name of Jesus Christ.

And from the days of John the Baptist until now the kingdom of heaven suffereth violence, and the violent take it by force.

Matthew 11:12 KJV

Face the Devil Head On

I rebuke and bind every astral-projecting person who is trying to infiltrate my home. I cut off every assignment of the devil and his demons that is trying to destroy me, in the name of Jesus.

They spread a net for my feet—I was bowed down in distress. They dug a pit in my path—but they have fallen into it themselves.

Psalm 57:6 NIV

In the name of Jesus, I send Holy Ghost fire upon every spirit of infirmity that is attacking my body.

That power is the same as the mighty strength he exerted when he raised Christ from the dead.

Ephesians 1:19–20 NIV

Face the Devil Head On

I break down and dismantle every satanic altar that has my picture or my clothing or my hair—I smash them down now with the blood of Jesus Christ.

Evening, morning and noon I cry out in distress, and he hears my voice. He rescues me unharmed from the battle waged against me, even though many oppose me.

Psalm 55:17–18 NIV

Face the Devil Head On

Father, I take back in the name of Jesus everything that the cankerworm and the locust have eaten from my life and my loved ones' lives. I pour fire upon every devil's head and every unclean spirit and every witch who has risen up against my family, my finances, my church and me. I smite them with the blood of Jesus seven times and destroy them, never to rise again, in Jesus' name.

O God, shatter their teeth in their mouth.

Psalm 58:6 NASB

Face the Devil Head On

I rebuke and dismantle every plan or insight that the devil and his demons have against me. Let them be destroyed, in Jesus' name.

The LORD will take vengeance on his adversaries.

Nahum 1:2 KJV

Face the Devil Head On

I shut down every whisper, and I shut down every lie of the devil and his cronies against me, because the Word of the Lord says I am more than a conqueror in Christ Jesus. So, Satan, I resist you in the name of Jesus Christ.

In all these things we are more than conquerors through him that loved us.

Romans 8:37 KJV

Face the Devil Head On

I call the fire of God to fall upon the enemy's camp and destroy every demonic altar that has my name on it, in Jesus' name. I send arrows dipped in the blood of Jesus Christ into the enemy's camp right now, in Jesus' name.

> "Thus says the Lord GOD, . . . 'You were the anointed cherub who covers . . . until unrighteousness was found in you. . . . By the multitude of your iniquities, in the unrighteousness of your trade you profaned your sanctuaries. Therefore I have brought fire from the midst of you; it has consumed you, and I have turned you to ashes on the earth in the eyes of all who see you.'"
>
> Ezekiel 28:12, 14–15, 18 NASB

Face the Devil Head On

I burn down the banners and scrolls of any evil plan against me and my family and my ministry, in Jesus' name. I send confusion into the enemy's camp right now, in Jesus' name.

Confuse them, Lord, and frustrate their plans.

Psalm 55:9 NLT

Face the Devil Head On

I will not entertain, I will not listen to and I will not obey the lies of the enemy. And I will proclaim the blessings of the Lord upon my life in every season. I will live and not die, and I will confess these blessings upon my life today for my family, for the season I am in, for my purpose and for my destiny.

Keep me as the apple of Your eye; hide me under the shadow of Your wings, from the wicked who oppress me, from my deadly enemies who surround me. . . . As for me, I will see Your face in righteousness; I shall be satisfied when I awake in Your likeness.

Psalm 17:8–9, 15 NKJV

Face the Devil Head On

I pray that God's supernatural knowledge of His truth be engrafted into my spirit and my heart. And I pray that I will fulfill my life's purpose, with no hindrances or delays, in Jesus' name.

God from the beginning chose you for salvation through sanctification by the Spirit and belief in the truth.

2 Thessalonians 2:13 NKJV

PART 8

STAND STRONG IN BATTLE

JOURNALING SPACE

Jesus declared to our brother Peter a statement so powerful that it shook the gates of hell and blew the doors wide open. He said, "Upon this rock I will build my church; and the gates of hell shall not prevail against it" (Matthew 16:18 KJV).

The last time I checked, I *am* the Church of Jesus Christ. So, devil, get out of my way or get run over, in Jesus' name.

Stand Strong in Battle

Lord, look at the attacks from the enemy upon Your Church and release the fire of Your Spirit upon them.

God has put all things under the authority of Christ and has made him head over all things for the benefit of the church.

Ephesians 1:22 NLT

Stand Strong in Battle

I release arrows dipped in the blood of Jesus into the enemy's camp to destroy every satanic target that opposes the Church of Jesus. Let them be destroyed in the name of Jesus.

For this purpose the Son of God was manifested, that he might destroy the works of the devil.

1 John 3:8 KJV

Stand Strong in Battle

I speak by the authority and power of the Holy Spirit. Let every witch that has infiltrated the Church of Jesus Christ from the north, south, east and west be removed, in Jesus' name.

"The people will hear and be afraid. . . . Fear and dread will fall on them; by the greatness of Your arm they will be as still as a stone, till Your people pass over, O Lord, till the people pass over whom you have purchased."

Exodus 15:14, 16 NKJV

Stand Strong in Battle

I frustrate the plans, devices, schemes and wiles of the devil, as well as the plans, devices and schemes of any witches or warlocks that have been assigned to afflict the Church. I uproot them in the name of Jesus.

O Lord, the hope of Israel, all who turn away from you will be disgraced. They will be buried in the dust of the earth, for they have abandoned the Lord, the fountain of living water.

Jeremiah 17:13 NLT

Stand Strong in Battle

Let the silver cord used by any person from the dark side for astral projection into the Church be cut off in the name of Jesus.

This is what the Lord says: "Cursed is the one . . . whose heart turns away from the Lord. That person . . . will dwell in the parched places of the desert, in a salt land where no one lives."

Jeremiah 17:5–6 NIV

Stand Strong in Battle

I smite with the blood of Jesus seven times any witches who are infiltrating church services and releasing incantations upon the congregations and leaders. Be removed now in the name of Jesus.

The Lord is good, a stronghold in the day of trouble; he knows those who take refuge in him. But with an overflowing flood he will make a complete end of the adversaries, and will pursue his enemies into darkness.

Nahum 1:7–8 ESV

Any animal sacrifices of any witches against the Church of Jesus Christ, or any demonic altars that have been set up, I destroy them all with the blood of Jesus and the finished work of the cross.

[The false prophets] cried with a loud voice and cut themselves according to their custom with swords and lances until the blood gushed out on them . . . but . . . no one answered.

1 Kings 18:28–29 NASB

Stand Strong in Battle

With the blood of Jesus, I smite to ashes any articles the witches have stolen that represent the Church and its mission statement.

The Lord has given commandment about [His foes]: . . . "From the house of your gods I will cut off the carved image and the metal image. I will make your grave, for you are vile."

Nahum 1:14 ESV

Stand Strong in Battle

Any and all witchcraft planting or burials against the Church of Jesus Christ, I destroy in the name of Jesus.

Behold, the wicked man conceives evil. . . . He makes a pit, digging it out, and falls into the hole that he has made.

Psalm 7:14–15 ESV

Stand Strong in Battle

I call upon the Lord to release warring angels from Michael's quarters to dismantle and uproot any witchcraft network in my region. May they be destroyed from the north, south, east and west.

"Look, you scoffers, be astounded and perish; for I am doing a work in your days, a work that you will not believe, even if one tells it to you."

Acts 13:41 ESV

I release the ten plagues of Jesus to fall upon every witch, wizard, sorcerer and warlock who is infiltrating the Church of Jesus Christ.

[Jesus] disarmed the spiritual rulers and authorities. He shamed them publicly by his victory over them on the cross.

Colossians 2:15 NLT

Stand Strong in Battle

For all the witches who are chanting, casting spells and astral projecting against the Church of Jesus Christ, I bind every dark work and turn it against their own heads until they repent in the name of Jesus.

His mischief will return upon his own head, and his violence will descend upon his own pate.

Psalm 7:16 NASB

I break and uproot every scheme, pattern and cycle of witchcraft designed to stop the growth of the Church. I destroy them all by the blood of Jesus Christ, in Jesus' name.

It is a righteous thing with God to repay with tribulation those who trouble you.

2 Thessalonians 1:6 NKJV

Stand Strong in Battle

I send confusion into the enemy's camp. I confuse their languages. Let any and all who are trying to bring down the Church of Jesus Christ attack one another.

The wicked will perish; and the enemies of the LORD will . . . vanish—like smoke they vanish away.

Psalm 37:20 NASB

I forbid any witchcraft meetings from taking place in any region where the Church is planted. May the fire of the Holy Spirit fall upon their heads, in the name of Jesus.

Every morning I will put to silence all the wicked in the land; I will cut off every evildoer from the city of the Lord.

Psalm 101:8 NIV

Stand Strong in Battle

I destroy and curse at the root every witchcraft spell against the Church of Jesus Christ. Let it be destroyed, in Jesus' name.

You shall not be afraid of the terror by night, nor of the arrow that flies by day.

Psalm 91:5 NKJV

Stand Strong in Battle

I destroy every witchcraft covering and covenant from the first and second heavens and dismantle the operation piece by piece, never to rise up again against the Church of Jesus Christ.

The weapons of our warfare are not of the flesh but have divine power to destroy strongholds.

2 Corinthians 10:3–4 ESV

I release the bondages of heaven to chase down every witch, warlock, wizard or sorcerer who is standing against the Church of Jesus Christ. I declare this in Jesus' name.

They close up their callous hearts, and their mouths speak with arrogance. . . . Rise up, LORD, confront them, bring them down.

Psalm 17:10, 13 NIV

Let the path of every devil and every witch assigned against the Church be slippery, and let them spiral out of control to destroy themselves, in Jesus' name.

Let those be ashamed and dishonored who seek my life; let those be turned back and humiliated who devise evil against me. Let them be like chaff before the wind, with the angel of the Lord driving them on.

Psalm 35:4–6 NASB

I go into the devil's camp and take back every blessing that he stole from the Church through witchcraft. I take it all back in the name of Jesus.

"There will be peace for the seed: the vine will yield its fruit, the land will yield its produce and the heavens will give their dew; and I will cause the remnant of this people to inherit all these things. . . . I will save you that you may become a blessing. Do not fear; let your hands be strong."

Zechariah 8:12–13 NASB

Stand Strong in Battle

In the name of Jesus Christ, I loose the hands and feet of every believer in the Church to walk out and evangelize.

The night is far spent, the day is at hand: . . . let us put on the armour of light.

Romans 13:12 KJV

PART 9

RELEASE THE THUNDER OF GOD

JOURNALING SPACE

Do not make it easy for the devil by giving him so much credit when he is a defeated foe. I remember when I was living on the other side of the cross how I used to live dangerously (spiritually speaking). In all of my battles, I did not let the other person breathe or take a time out or go on vacation. I worked consistently to get my victory. I pushed back in demonic spiritual warfare.

How much more should I push back today, now that I am on the other side of the cross, knowing that Jesus Christ has won the victory and handed me the keys to the Kingdom? He has made me a victor in spiritual warfare, and He has done this same thing for you.

As you pray these prayers, you will be asking the Father for the thunderbolts of Jehovah Nissi to strike the head of every snake that has risen up against you, and you will be binding up every unclean spirit that is working against you.

Release the Thunder of God

I release the thunder of God against every target that has my name on it in the enemy's camp: Be destroyed now!

"The adversaries of the Lord shall be broken in pieces; from heaven He will thunder against them."

1 Samuel 2:10 NKJV

I release the rod of God to torment every demon that has been assigned against me. I release the plagues of Egypt on the head of every devil that is trying to steal my anointing, my purpose and my destiny.

It is a terrifying thing to fall into the hands of the living God.

Hebrews 10:31 NASB

I send hailstorms upon every head of every demon that is attacking me. I release hornets to attack every devil, witch and warlock that rises up against me. I send out the hound dogs of heaven to chase down every devil and torment them, until they release my blessing.

"Your right hand, O Lord, shatters the enemy."

Exodus 15:6 NASB

Release the Thunder of God

I send an earthquake into the enemy's camp to destroy and bring down every satanic altar that has been set up against me, my family, my loved ones, my ministry and all that belongs to me.

"You raised you right hand, and the earth swallowed our enemies."

Exodus 15:12 NLT

With the sword of the Lord, I will chop off the head of every evil spirit the same way David took off the head of Goliath. In Jesus' name, I pluck out the eyes of every evil spirit operating through witches, wizards, sorcerers and warlocks that has been assigned to spy on my life.

And it came to pass, when they brought out those kings unto Joshua, that Joshua called for all the men of Israel, and said unto the captains of the men of war which went with him, Come near, put your feet upon the necks of these kings. And they came near, and put their feet upon the necks of them.

Joshua 10:24 KJV

I ask God to release blindness into the enemy's camp and cut off every circuit that is trying to infiltrate my purpose and destiny. I bring them down and destroy them completely through the power of the Holy Spirit, in Jesus' name.

As the enemy came down toward him, Elisha prayed to the LORD, "Strike this army with blindness." So he struck them with blindness, as Elisha had asked.

2 Kings 6:18 NIV

I hinder and frustrate every assignment of the devil and his demons and whatever methods they are trying to use against me. I burn them down with the fire of the Holy Spirit.

Our God is a consuming fire.

Hebrews 12:29 KJV

I shoot lightning into the devil's camp and upon every demon's head, to confuse and destroy their game plan against my life, in Jesus' name.

The way of the wicked is like total darkness.
They have no idea what they are stumbling over.

Proverbs 4:19 NLT

Release the Thunder of God

I bind and rebuke all demonic reinforcements sent by the evil one to attack, hinder or frustrate the plan of God over my life. I dismantle them in the name of Jesus.

"Is not My word like a fire?" says the Lord, "and like a hammer that breaks the rock in pieces?"

Jeremiah 23:29 NKJV

Release the Thunder of God

I bind up principalities and powers, rulers of the darkness of this world, spiritual wickedness and hosts in high places, and the prince of power of the air over my region, and I command you to release and loose my family, every church in my area and me now, in Jesus' name.

Why do the nations conspire and the peoples plot in vain? The kings of the earth rise up and the rulers band together against the LORD and against his anointed. . . . The One enthroned in heaven laughs; the Lord scoffs at them. He rebukes them in his anger and terrifies them in his wrath, saying, "I have installed my king on Zion, my holy mountain."

Psalm 2:1–2, 4–6 NIV

I bind up the strong man and the old man and every stronghold of every demonic spirit that is trying to plague and confuse my loved ones and me, in Jesus' name.

[Jesus said,] "If I cast out demons by the finger of God, then the kingdom of God has come upon you. When a strong man, fully armed, guards his own house, his possessions are undisturbed. But when someone stronger than he attacks him and overpowers him, he takes away form him all his armor on which he had relied and distributes his plunder."

Luke 11:20–22 NASB

I bind up every spirit of fear, doubt, unbelief, discouragement, despair or depression that is trying to come against me, along with the spirits of pride, rebellion, disobedience, ego, independence, lack of forgiveness, bitterness and lust. I come against all lying, seducing or deceiving spirits that are trying to attack me. I send judgments of God upon their heads, in Jesus' name.

[Jesus is] far above all rule and authority and power and dominion, and every name that is named, not only in this age but also in the one to come.

Ephesians 1:21 NASB

Release the Thunder of God

I bind up any spirit of envy, covetousness, jealousy, lust of the eyes, lust of the world, pride of life, spirit of mammon, spirits of pity and hopelessness, and every other wicked unclean spirit that accompanies these spirits, in Jesus' name.

The seventy returned with joy, saying, "Lord, even the demons are subject to us in Your name."

Luke 10:17 NASB

Release the Thunder of God

I bind up the spirits of infirmity, sickness, disease, pain, addiction, affliction, calamity and premature death that are trying to operate against my loved ones and me. I bind up every attack that is operating in my immune system, every accident spirit and every demonic spirit that is trying to abort my purpose and destiny. I cut them at the root, never to return, in Jesus' name.

Because you have made the LORD, who is my refuge, even the Most High, your dwelling place, no evil shall befall you, nor shall any plague come near your dwelling; for He shall give His angels charge over you.

Psalm 91:9–11 NKJV

I come against, in the name of Jesus, every spirit of poverty that is trying to steal my promises and blessings. I dismantle them in the name of Jesus. I bind up the spirits of strife and division, backbiting, gossip, criticism and judgment. I smite them with the blood of Jesus seven times and break myself free from them, in Jesus' name.

The reason the Son of God appeared was to destroy the works of the devil.

1 John 3:8 ESV

I bind up the spirits of resistance, hindrance, revenge, retaliation and retribution that are trying to come against my family, my ministry and me, in Jesus' name.

[The destructive ones] band themselves together against the life of the righteous. . . . But the Lord has been my stronghold, and my God the rock of my refuge. He has brought back their wickedness upon them and will destroy them in their evil; the Lord our God will destroy them.

Psalm 94:21–23 NASB

In the name of Jesus, I bind up every root of fear, anxiety, worry, stress, tension, frustration, disappointment and discouragement. I bind up all these devils that are working against me, in the name of Jesus.

Every valley shall be exalted, and every mountain and hill shall be made low: and the crooked shall be made straight, and the rough places plain.

Isaiah 40:4 KJV

In Jesus' name, I take authority over all curses that have been spoken over my life. I renounce and loose myself from every demonic dedication placed upon my life.

Now the LORD said to Abram, . . . "I will bless those who bless you, and the one who curses you I will curse."

Genesis 12:1, 3 NASB

I bind up in the name of Jesus every tongue that rises against me, and I condemn it in judgment. I bind up every snare or trap of the evil one that is trying to operate against me, in Jesus' name. May the Lord Jesus Christ rebuke you all.

"No weapon that is fashioned against [the righteous] shall succeed, and you shall refute every tongue that rises against you in judgment. This is the heritage of the servants of the Lord and their vindication from me, declares the Lord."

Isaiah 54:17 ESV

PART 10

COVER OUR YOUNG PEOPLE IN PRAYER

JOURNALING SPACE

*I*f we are not careful, history will repeat itself. My childhood and younger years—and even part of my adult life—were robbed from me because I was given over to the dark side. Today, in my travels as an evangelist, I thank God that He has allowed me to minister to so many young people in the most critical seasons of their lives, so that what happened to me will not happen to them.

One thing you will notice as you dig into God's Word is that many of the people God called in the Old Testament were young. Esther was young, Ruth was young, Joseph was young, David was young, Daniel was young and the three Hebrew boys were young. We should never neglect or bypass young people, many of whom are in the grips of Satan because of doors that have been opened in their lives.

From the time they are born, children are targets that the enemy goes the extra mile to capture. Do not be surprised at this startling reality. Instead, I hope this truth puts enough fight in you to rise up in Kingdom faith to snatch our young people back from the devil's clutches.

Cover Our Young People in Prayer

Today in the name of Jesus, I serve the devil notice to loose our young people.

> Thus says the Lord GOD: "Behold, I will lift up my hand to the nations, and raise my signal to the peoples; and they shall bring your sons in their arms, and your daughters shall be carried on their shoulders."
>
> Isaiah 49:22 ESV

Cover Our Young People in Prayer

I break every demonic attack, every tormenting spirit, every suicidal spirit, every cutting spirit, every emotional demon, every sexual demon, every rape spirit, every molestation spirit, every abandonment spirit, the spirit of rejection, every tormenting and scorning spirit of the mind—I break your powers and grip over our children and young people now, in the name of Jesus.

"All your children will be taught by the LORD, and great will be their peace."

Isaiah 54:13 NIV

Cover Our Young People in Prayer

Any spirit that has come into our young people through the eye gates by watching horror movies, pornography or media and games with witchcraft or spiritualism or anything else ungodly, I destroy your powers, in the name of Jesus.

The LORD, my refuge, even the Most High, [is] your dwelling place. . . . You will not be afraid of the terror by night, or of the arrow that flies by day; of the pestilence that stalks in darkness, or of the destruction that lays waste at noon.

Psalm 91:9, 5–6 NASB

Cover Our Young People in Prayer

Any demonic spirits that have come through family bloodlines, I destroy your powers against our young people in the name of Jesus. Any transfer of spirits of any kind, I sever and cut you at the root and command you to leave now, in Jesus' name.

"[My people] shall dwell in the land that I have given to Jacob My servant . . . and they shall dwell there, they, their children, and their children's children, forever."

Ezekiel 37:25 NKJV

Cover Our Young People in Prayer

Any premature death spirits, lying, deceiving and seductive spirits, any alcohol spirits and any pharmakeia *spirits attacking our young people, I rip you apart in the name of Jesus. Leave now, in Jesus' name.*

This is what the Lord says: "Yes, captives will be taken from warriors, and plunder retrieved from the fierce; I will contend with those who contend with you, and your children I will save."

Isaiah 49:25 NIV

Cover Our Young People in Prayer

I bind every spirit that has caused division in our young people's minds, bodies, souls and spirits. I call back every piece from the enemy's camp. I call back from the north, south, east and west, in Jesus' name.

"It is not the will of your Father which is in heaven, that one of these little ones should perish."

Matthew 18:14 KJV

Cover Our Young People in Prayer

I seal our children and young people in the blood of Jesus Christ, and I release the judgments of God upon the devil.

See, the Sovereign LORD comes with power, and he rules with a mighty arm. . . . He tends his flock like a shepherd: He gathers the lambs in his arms and carries them close to his heart.

Isaiah 40:10–11 NIV

Cover Our Young People in Prayer

I ask God to release angels from Michael's quarters to arrest every devil working against our young people, never to return, in Jesus' name, Amen.

"O my God . . . the children of your people will live in security. Their children's children will thrive in your presence."

Psalm 102:24, 28 NLT

Cover Our Young People in Prayer

I seal every young person I know in the words of Psalm 91 and in the blood of Jesus.

Jesus said, "Let the little children come to Me."
Matthew 19:14 NKJV

PART 11

LOOSE GOD'S BLESSINGS OVER YOUR LIFE

JOURNALING SPACE

I learned through a well-known TV preacher that a ship can make it through any storm as long as the water does not get in. In the same way, you as a believer can go through anything in life as long as the situation or the storm does not overtake *you*.

Strengthen your position in spiritual storms. Speak these words of blessing over your life.

Loose God's Blessings over Your Life

I loose over me in the mighty name of Jesus Christ freedom, liberation, peace, joy, hope, gladness, love, healing, wholeness, nothing missing and nothing broken, mercy, grace, blessings and favor, and restoration of all the years the locusts and the cankerworms have eaten.

"I, the LORD, have rebuilt the ruined places and planted what was desolate. I, the LORD, have spoken it, and I will do it."

Ezekiel 36:36 NKJV

Loose God's Blessings over Your Life

I loose an open heaven over my life in the name of Jesus. I loose love, meekness, obedience and kindness upon myself now. I loose compassion, consideration for others, submissiveness and divine healing into my life.

All who are led by the Spirit of God are sons of God.

Romans 8:14 ESV

Loose God's Blessings over Your Life

I loose the desires of my heart, according to the purpose of Jesus Christ, over my life.

"Sing about a fruitful vineyard: I, the LORD, watch over it; I water it continually. I guard it day and night so that no on may harm it."

Isaiah 27:2–3 NIV

Loose God's Blessings over Your Life

I loose the blessings and promises of the Lord upon my life, family, ministry and home. I speak and loose breakthrough in every area of my life. May a double portion of God's blessing be upon me, my family, my home and my ministry, now in Jesus' name.

This is the message from the LORD. . . . I promise this very day that I will repay two blessings for each of your troubles.

Zechariah 9:1, 12 NLT

Loose God's Blessings over Your Life

In the name of Jesus, I loose promotion, breakthrough, restoration and restitution over my life.

The LORD their God will save his people on that day as a shepherd saves his flock. They will sparkle in his land like jewels in a crown. How attractive and beautiful they will be!

Zechariah 9:16–17 NIV

Loose God's Blessings over Your Life

I loose a hedge of protection over my mind, over my heart and over my emotions in Jesus' name. Thank You, Jesus, always.

He led his own people like a flock of sheep, guiding them safely through the wilderness. He kept them safe so they were not afraid.

Psalm 78:52–53 NLT

Father, I thank You and praise You for a fresh anointing that will keep me every day of my life. I give You the entire honor, all the praise and worship, in the unmatchable name of Your Son, Jesus Christ.

In the beginning was the Word, and the Word was with God, and the Word was God. He was with God in the beginning. Through him all things were made; without him nothing was made that has been made. In him was life, and that life was the light of all mankind. The light shines in the darkness, and the darkness has not overcome it.

John 1:1–5 NIV

PART 12

WALK IN VICTORY

JOURNALING SPACE

God has so much for us today. We should give the devil something to think twice about when he tries to trespass into our spiritual territory against our ministries, against our finances, against our health and against our families and homes. We are equipped to cage up these devils once and for all never to return, to set the judgment of God upon their heads and to ask God to release holy angels to fight on our behalf.

If you apply and live out these spiritual weapons in your Christian walk, you will never see a day in the valley of dry bones. That does not mean you will not face the evil one. You will—you can count on it—but you will always have the victory.

Before I was formed in my mother's womb, God already had a plan for me. I am not a mistake.

You have searched me, LORD, and you know me.... You are familiar with all my ways.... For you created my inmost being; you knit me together in my mother's womb. I praise you because I am fearfully and wonderfully made; your works are wonderful, I know that full well.... All the day ordained for me were written in your book before one of them came to be.

Psalm 139:1, 3, 13–14, 16 NIV

Walk in Victory

I am the righteousness of God through Christ Jesus. I am a citizen in God's Kingdom through Jesus Christ and the finished work of the cross.

The LORD loves the gates of Zion. . . . Glorious things are spoken of you, O city of God. . . . The LORD will count when He registers the peoples: "This one was born there."

Psalm 87:2, 6 NASB

I am the head and not the tail. I am above and not beneath. I can do all things through Christ Jesus, who gives me the strength.

"If you listen to these commands of the Lord your God . . . and if you carefully obey them, the Lord will make you the head and not the tail, and you will always be on top and never at the bottom."

Deuteronomy 28:13 NLT

Walk in Victory

Greater is He who lives in me than he who lives in the world. My body is the temple of the Holy Spirit.

Don't you realize that your body is the temple of the Holy Spirit, who lives in you and was given to you by God? You do not belong to yourself.

1 Corinthians 6:19 NLT

Walk in Victory

I am blessed with all spiritual blessings in Christ Jesus.

After these things I looked, and behold, a great multitude which no one could count, from every nation and all tribes and peoples and tongues, standing before the throne and before the Lamb, clothed in white robes, and palm branches were in their hands; and they cry out with a loud voice, saying, "Salvation to our God who sits on the throne, and to the Lamb." And all the angels were standing around the throne and around the elders and the four living creatures; and they fell on their faces before the throne and worshiped God, saying, "Amen, blessing and glory and wisdom and thanksgiving and honor and power and might, be to our God forever and ever. Amen."

Revelation 7:9–12 NASB

A Final Word

By boldly praying the prayers in this book with me, you have learned to crush the enemy whenever he advances against you. Refer to these prayers often to keep your heart and mind fresh for battle. We as the Church must fight for our Promised Land. We fight for our purpose, our destiny, our salvation, our families, our loved ones and even the unbelievers in the world so they, too, can have an opportunity to make it to the cross. We are soldiers and ambassadors of an army so elite that words cannot adequately describe it.

It is reality in a battle with such a powerful enemy that at times you will feel spiritually weak, exhausted in a hundred ways, even tasting discouragement. You must learn to push your way through in the power of the Holy Spirit, and then, like the woman with the

A Final Word

issue of blood, touch the hem of Jesus' garment and get your victory.

Never, ever let the devil trick you into believing that the battle is too strong for you. When Jesus Christ wakes me up every morning, I know the devil is in trouble. I am God's secret weapon. And so are you. Let us thank Jesus together. Thank You, Jesus!

As you continue to walk forward in the power of the name of Jesus, into the promises He has for you, hold fast to these truths:

- You have a personal relationship with God and serve Him alone.
- Your life has purpose and destiny, so never buy into the lies of the devil.
- Storms do not last. Do not make permanent decisions in temporary situations.
- It often helps you in battle to take inventory and assess your spiritual walk. Examine the season you are in and the season you are entering into so that the devil will not trip you up.
- It is not important what the devil throws at you. What is important is what you do about it in Christ.

A Final Word

- Living every day as if it were your last, in Jesus Christ, will help you keep your focus in warfare.
- Continue to grow strong as a spiritual sniper praying combat prayers. The devil will not stand a chance against you.

John Ramirez is an internationally known evangelist, author and highly sought-out speaker who shares the story of how he was trained to be a priest in a satanic cult (Santeria and spiritualism), casting powerful witchcraft spells and controlling entire regions.

For almost twenty years, Ramirez has been teaching believers around the globe—from cities across the United States and the Virgin Islands to Germany, the United Kingdom and Japan—how to defeat the enemy. He has appeared on broadcasts such as *The 700 Club*, TBN, The Word Network and The Church Channel.

In his first book, *Out of the Devil's Cauldron: A Journey from Darkness to Light*, Ramirez tells of his early training to become a warlock, eventually ranking as the third highest devil worshiper in New York City. In his gritty, transparent style, he walks you through the dark alleys of the Santeria cult while exposing hidden secrets of darkness. He unfolds God's enormous power through his testimony and teaches Christians as well as those trapped in the occult how to combat the enemy and be set free.

Ramirez grew up in an impoverished ghetto neighborhood, despising his father for his careless disregard of his family. He learned quickly how to survive the cold, harsh streets of the South Bronx. But in his search for love and validation, he found acceptance in a new "family" of witches and warlocks who groomed him to become a high priest in their occult religion. His plunge into the dark side reached a boiling point on the night he sold his soul to the devil in a diabolical, blood-soaked ritual.

With renewed fervor—and the mark of the beast now cut into his right arm—he actively recruited souls into this unholy kingdom, haunting the bars and clubs of New York City by night to find his next victims. His life continued down this dark path until God intervened through a miraculous, larger-than-life dream, revealing Himself for who He really is and literally snatching Ramirez from the grips of hell.

According to Ramirez, people from all ethnic backgrounds dabble in the occult and fall victim to this satanic underworld and never see the way out. He is one in a million who made it out.